1001
Things to Spot
in
Fairyland

Gillian Doherty
Illustrated by Teri Gower

Designed by Teri Gower and Doriana Berkovic
Edited by Anna Milbourne

Contents

Things to spot

Fairyland is a magical place where just about anything can happen, and often does. Each scene in this book has all kinds of wonderful and surprising things for you to find and count. There are 1001 things to spot altogether.

Fairy palace

10 stripy fish

7 spotty turtles

10 pink flags

8 mermaids

7 boats with leaf sails

8 nutshell boats

10 fairy horses

9 elf archers

6 pearls

8 goblin guards

16

17

Each little picture shows you what to look for in the big picture.

The pink number tells you how many of that thing you need to find.

Dizzy Rainbow is new in fairyland and is busy exploring and discovering its secrets. Can you find her in every scene?

Fairy feast

10 leaf trays

9 bowls of marshmallows

10 sugar mice

9 blackberry tarts

8 yellow bows

7 paper garlands

10 strawberry drinks

9 fairy cakes

1 greedy goblin

8 plates of star cookies

Enchanted waterfall

10 rainbow fish

8 yellow frogs

5 fairies in hammocks

9 flying fish

10 emeralds

2 kingfishers

3 fairies washing their hair

5 mirrors

7 treasure chests

6 elves diving for jewels

Moon dance

7 shooting stars

10 white rabbits

6 pixies on toadstools

1 full moon

9 fairies with sparkly wings

2 golden slippers

10 fairy lanterns

2 snowy owls

8 glow-worms

1 unicorn

9

Fairy school

7 fairies having flying lessons

6 writing quills

10 purple beetles

3 pumpkin coaches

8 spell books

10 magic wands

9 white mice

5 frog princes

1 baby dragon

8 pink snails

Magic market

10 jars of fairy kisses

9 candy canes

7 petal parasols

8 magic lamps

7 rainbow cauldrons

8 spell scrolls   4 flying carpets   10 book worms   9 wizard hats   10 boxes of wishes

Secret garden

6 pink
flower fairies

 **10** dandelion clocks

 **4** fairies splashing

 **9** dragonflies

 **5** daisy chains

 **9** yellow butterflies

8 stripy caterpillars

 **10** bluebells

 **7** yellow flower fairies

 **8** elves riding snails

15

Fairy palace

10 stripy fish

7 spotty turtles

10 pink flags

8 mermaids

7 boats with leaf sails

8 nutshell boats

10 fairy horses

9 elf archers

6 pearls

8 goblin guards

House fairies

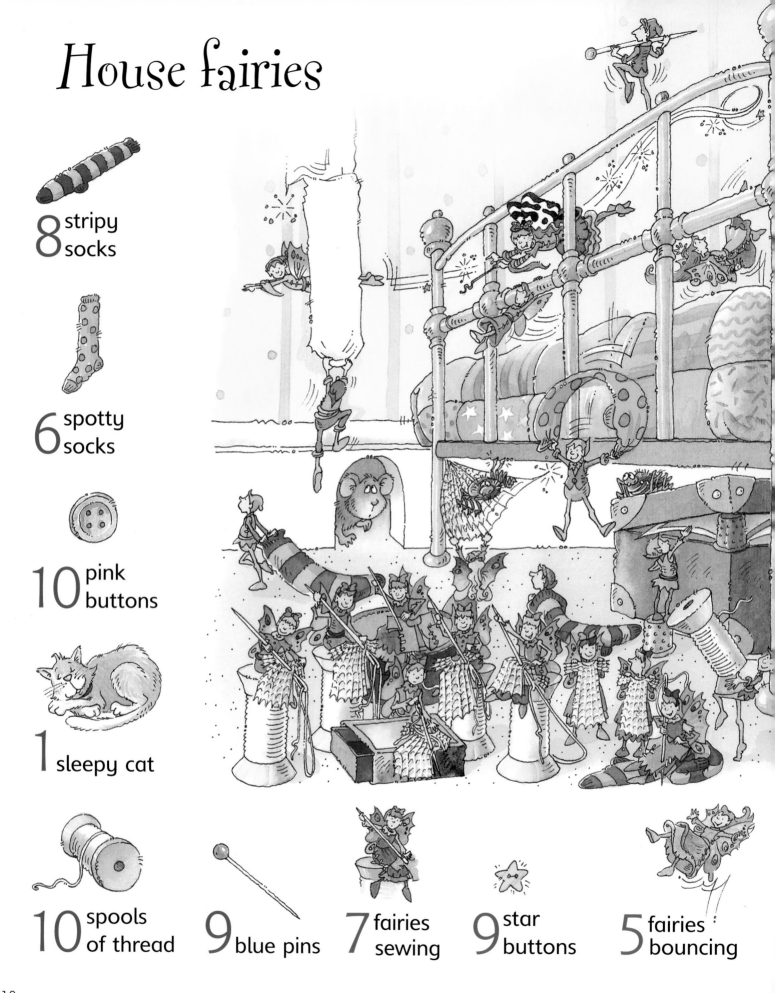

8 stripy socks

6 spotty socks

10 pink buttons

1 sleepy cat

10 spools of thread

9 blue pins

7 fairies sewing

9 star buttons

5 fairies bouncing

7 cobweb
dresses

Rainbow fairies

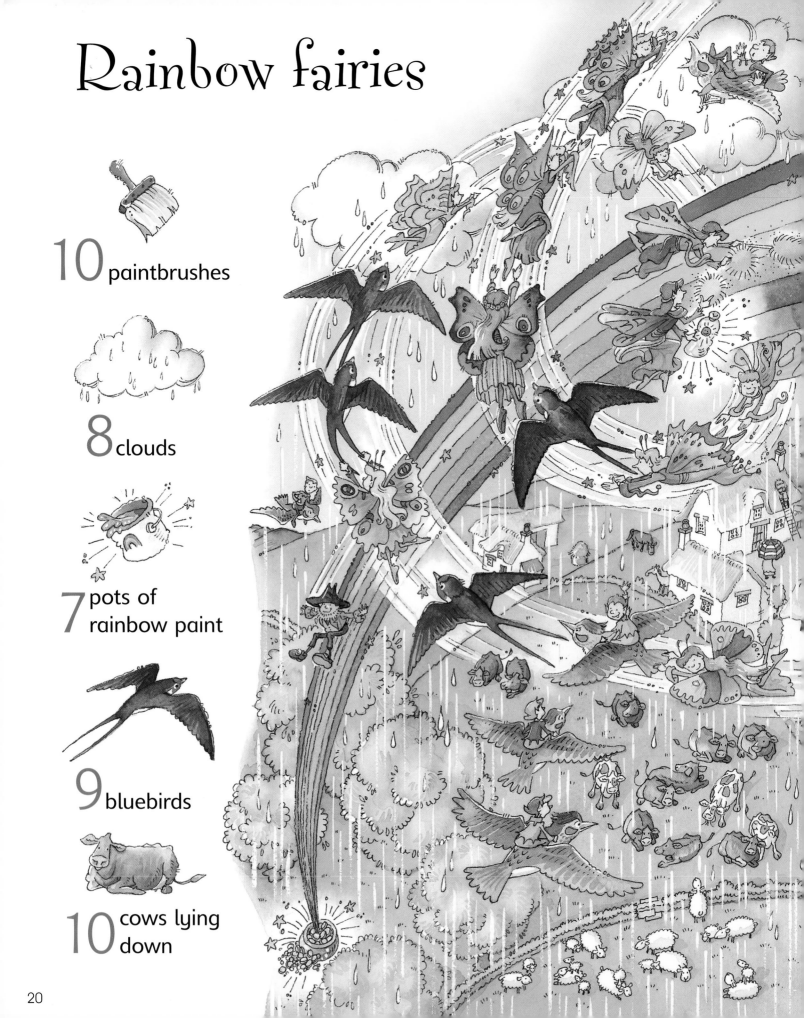

10 paintbrushes

8 clouds

7 pots of rainbow paint

9 bluebirds

10 cows lying down

1 leprechaun

8 stripy umbrellas

9 pixies riding on skylarks

1 pot of gold

10 chimney pots

Treetop fairies

2 red squirrels

5 pixies climbing ladders

9 moths

10 round windows

3 dormice sleeping

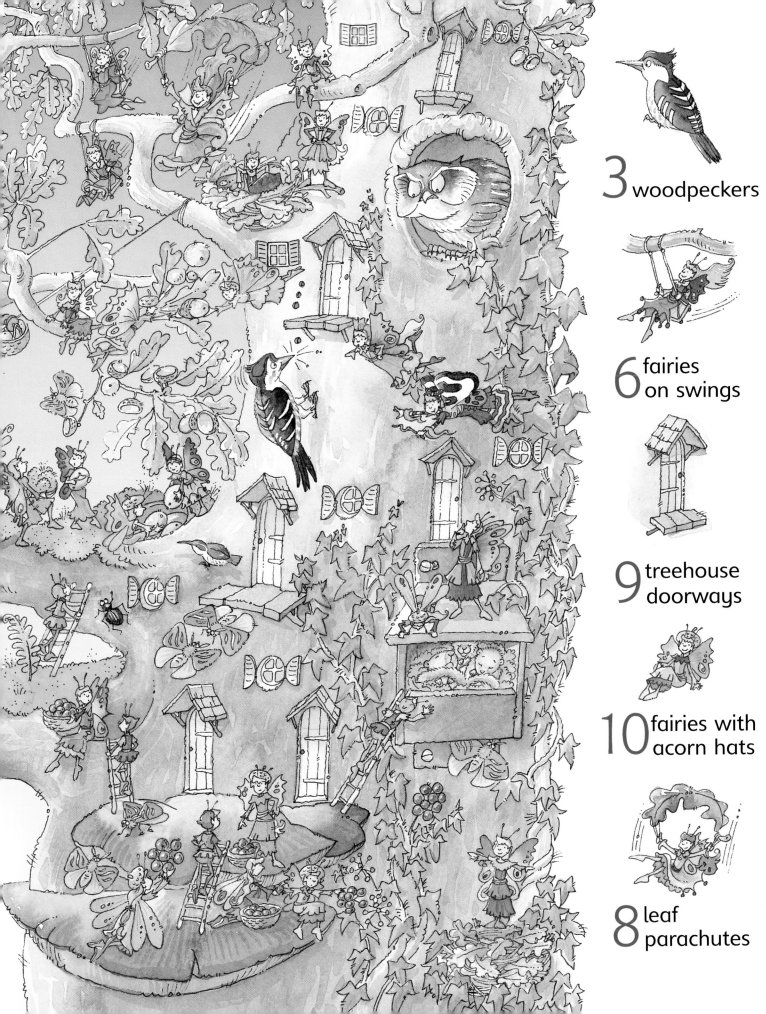

3 woodpeckers

6 fairies on swings

9 treehouse doorways

10 fairies with acorn hats

8 leaf parachutes

23

Fairy treehouse

9 candles

7 marbles

3 fairy newspapers

9 building blocks

8 feather dusters

6 baby fairies

4 self-flipping pancakes

1 pink rabbit

10 flyaway letters

2 snow fairies

Fairyland workshop

4 elves with red boxes

6 blue balloons

10 spotty bow ties

7 toy trains

9 fairy hammers

10 stripy balls

1 jack-in-a-box

3 fairies pulling levers

7 pouches of fairy dust

8 teddy bears

The Snow Queen's ball

7 fairies with fluffy hats

3 ice thrones

9 goblets of fairy punch

10 snowballs

3 golden crowns

2 golden bowls

8 red mittens

10 fairies ice-skating

1 crystal chandelier

7 snow hares

Dizzy Rainbow's magic spells

Dizzy Rainbow is just about to start fairy school.
She needs all kinds of strange things for her
magic class. Look back through the book
and see if you can help her find them all.

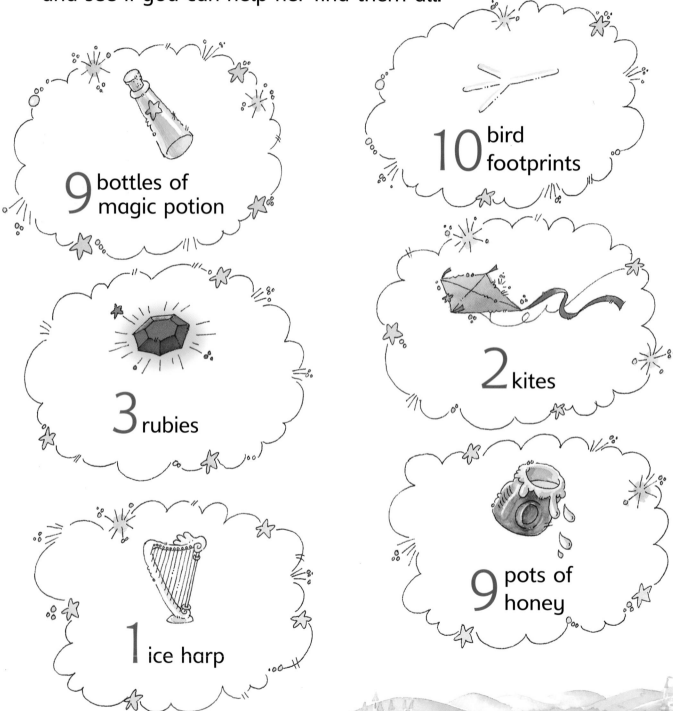

9 bottles of magic potion

10 bird footprints

3 rubies

2 kites

1 ice harp

9 pots of honey

10 bats

9 foxgloves

2 toads

10 buckets of raindrops

4 spiders

5 birds' nests

10 magic arrows

Answers

Did you find all the things Dizzy Rainbow needs for her magic class? Here's where they are:

9 bottles of magic potion:
Magic market
(pages 12–13)

9 pots of honey:
Fairy feast
(pages 4–5)

4 spiders:
House fairies
(pages 18–19)

10 bird footprints:
Fairy treehouse
(pages 24–25)

10 bats:
Moon dance
(pages 8–9)

5 birds' nests:
Treetop fairies
(pages 22–23)

3 rubies:
Enchanted waterfall
(pages 6–7)

9 foxgloves:
Secret garden
(pages 14–15)

10 magic arrows:
Fairy palace
(pages 16–17)

2 kites:
Fairyland workshop
(pages 26–27)

2 toads:
Fairy school
(pages 10–11)

1 ice harp:
The Snow Queen's ball
(pages 28–29)

10 buckets of raindrops:
Rainbow fairies
(pages 20–21)

First published in 2005 by Usborne Publishing Ltd.,
Usborne House, 83-85 Saffron Hill, London EC1N 8RT, England.
www.usborne.com